$10

A - 0

A/9

RUGS

BY JEFFREY WEISS

Photography by David Leach and Jon Elliott

W·W·NORTON & COMPANY
New York   London

For my Mother and Father

Design: Alix Serniak
Illustrations: Ken Druse
Cover photo: David Leach, home of Marion Larsen/Kent Ustin, San Francisco
Additional Photography by: J. Michael Kanouff, Nick Gunderson, Nancy Tobie, and Jeffrey Weiss
Rugs descriptions: George O. Bailey, Jr.

In addition to those whose homes are noted in the back of the book I wish to thank the many generous people who helped in the making of *Rugs.* Foremost is my editor, Ed Barber. As an editor I know how easy it is to obstruct and how difficult it is to facilitate. Ed helps. I am especially grateful to: Judith Carrington, Carla Cousins, Tom and Jane Doyle, Lila Gault, Joyce Goldstein, Betsy Groban, Trudy Kramer, John Loring, John Sloan, Karen McCreedy, Jim Roper, Peter Stamberg, Hannah Stuart, and Barbara Toll.

Published simultaneously in Canada by George J. McLeod Limited, Toronto.
Printed in the United States of America. All Rights Reserved.

First Edition

Library of Congress Cataloging in Publication Data

Weiss, Jeffrey.
    Rugs.

    1. Rugs in interior decoration.   I.   Title.
NK2115.5.R77F74   1979   747′.   79–13738
ISBN 0–393–01290–5
ISBN 0–393–00944–0 pbk.

1 2 3 4 5 6 7 8 9 0

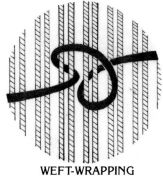

o other decorative touch can match the dramatic accent of a rug on a floor or wall, a rug that seems to be made for the space, whether it be a brilliant Persian, a fiery new Berber carpet from Morocco, a simple Shaker runner, or an exotic Chinese weave. *Rugs* is a panoramic visual report on how people of taste and style add an exuberant dimension to their homes with the addition of fabulous rugs.

With a few notable exceptions, all of the rugs pictured are unique. Each has been handmade with all the variety in weave, texture, pattern, and color that makes handcrafted objects so beautiful. Their individuality makes them exquisite. Even when they employ traditional stylized motifs and designs, there are differences — in the wool used, in the quality tightness of the knot, in the hues. Each has a personality.

The rugs in this book are not, by and large, examples of the fantastically priced carpets advertised at auction at Sotheby Parke Bernet. They are the selectively acquired "finishing touch" to a thoughtfully furnished home. They have been bought, over the years, by people on a budget. That is why there are so many kilims, or flat woven double-faced rugs. Since the western market was geared toward the pile or single-faced rug, flatweaves were not made for export until very recently. They therefore are now far more plentiful than their expensive plush brethren. Antique kilims can approach and even exceed in price other rugs, but it is far easier to buy a used, large, beautiful kilim in good condition for less than $1,000 than a small, damaged, ordinary antique pile carpet. To find how and where to buy rugs and for help in identifying the rugs shown in this book, I turned to George O. Bailey, Jr. Mr. Bailey, who has been collecting rugs for more than twenty

EXTRA-WEFT PATTERNING

SLIT TAPESTRY

WEFT-WRAPPING

TURKISH KNOT

PERSIAN KNOT

years, is a distinguished New York private dealer. He specializes in working with designers, architects, and private clients who engage him to find choice rugs. Mr. Bailey explains that it is highly unlikely that a tyro rug buyer will be able to make a sensible investment decision in rug purchase. For decades, knowledgeable dealers have roamed the auction and private markets here and abroad and there are many experts quick to spot a bargain. If you are contemplating purchasing a pile rug for less than $5,000 you are making an aesthetic not an investment decision. While it is true that oriental rugs show rapid appreciation, it is equally true that that appreciation is limited to fine quality examples. A good quality kilim is often available for thousands less. As with most purchases, well-placed confidence in the seller is your best assurance of fair dealing. Be especially wary of the new breed of nomad who pitches you and not his tent at a widely advertised motel auction of "superb collectors' rugs." Stick with a dealer who has been in business for some years and has a reputation to protect. For less expensive rugs, those in the $1,000 and under category, appearance and condition rather than any "antique" value are the primary concerns. Look for even wear and avoid extensively repaired rugs if you want them for floor use. Make sure that the binding and fringe are in good condition, that the backing (if the rug has a pile) is not cracked, and pay special attention to the condition of the wool. Be certain that it is not brittle. A good oriental rug can withstand hard wear for a great many years, but take some precautions. Always use a rug pad to cushion the blows of shoes and furniture. Attend to mothproofing and cleaning on a regular basis and don't use any of the chemical solvents sold in supermarkets or hardware stores to clean spots and stains. Let a professional rug cleaner do it.

But *Rugs* is not a practical guide. It is a continuation of the task I set for myself in *Made with Oak*, *Living Places*, and *Good Lives*, to document in an informal and decidedly idiosyncratic manner the pleasure that imaginative personal home decoration can bring to people of style, discernment, and of course, some means. I hope you enjoy the tour.

Jeffrey Weiss

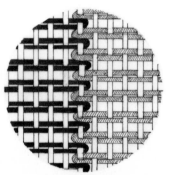

DOVE-TAILING

DOUBLE INTERLOCKING
(Reverse)

2

3

4

5

7

8

9

10

12

13

14

16

17

19

20

21

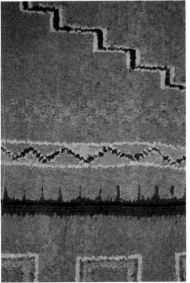

22

23

24

25

26

28

29

30

33

34

35

36

37

39

41

42

45

46

47

48

49

51

52

53

54

55

56

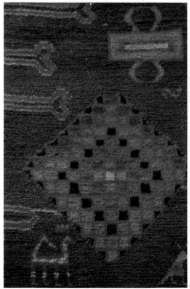

57

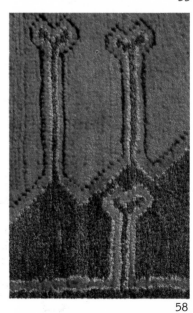

58

61

62

63

64

65

66

67

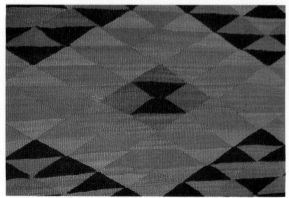

68

70

71

72

74

75

77

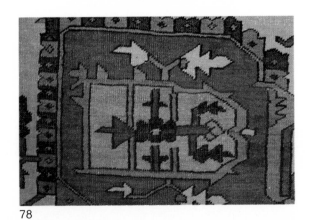

78

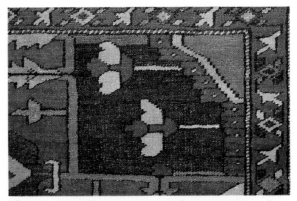

79

80

82

84

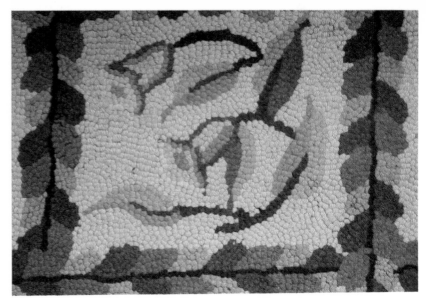

85

86

87

89

90

91

92

93

94

95

96

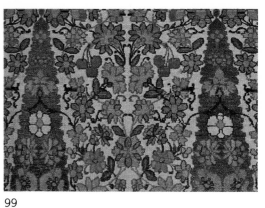

99

100

101

102

103

104

105

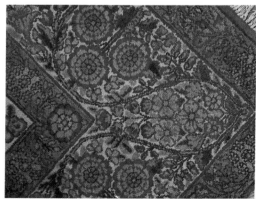

106

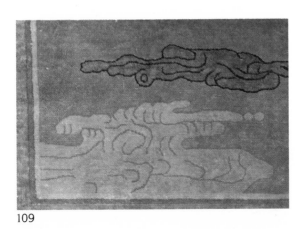

109

110

111

112

113

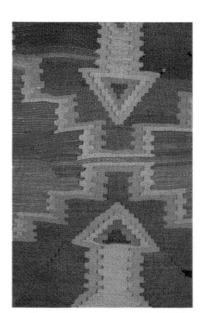

116

117

118

120

121

122

123

125

126

127

128

129

130

131

132

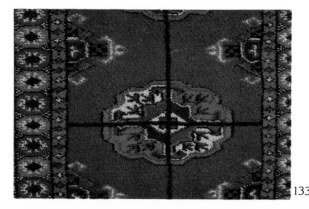

133

134

135

136

137

139

138

140

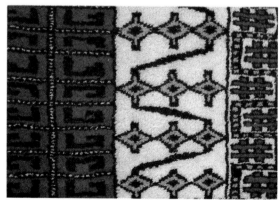

141

142

143

144

146

147

149

150

151

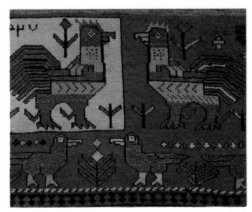

152

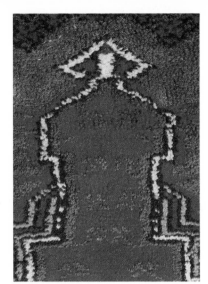

154

155

156

157

158

159

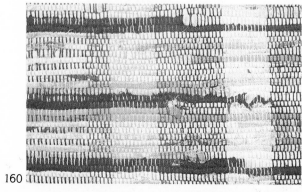

160

161

162

163

Credits

Captions

1   On floor left—Persian flatweave, late nineteenth century.

     On floor right—Persian pile rug, early twentieth century.

2   On floor—Southwest Persian (Fars) kilim, second half nineteenth century.

3   On floor—Pair of southwest Persian kilims joined together, late nineteenth century.

     Over piano—Persian kilim, late nineteenth century.

4   On floor—Persian kilim, late nineteenth century.

     Left wall—Caucasian pile rug, second half nineteenth century, Lesghi star design.

5   On floor—Persian kilim, early twentieth century.

     Also assorted Persian saddlebags made into pillows.

6   On floor—Persian (Qashqā'i) pile rug, late nineteenth century.

7   On floor—Anatolian kilim, early twentieth century.

8   On floor—Persian (Qashqā'i) pile rug, second half nineteenth century.

9   On floor—Anatolian prayer kilim, early twentieth century.

10 On floor—Persian (Qashqā'i area) pile rug of recent vintage.

11 On floor—Anatolian kilim, twentieth century, employing burgundy ground found so frequently in Turkish flatweaves.

12 On floor—Anatolian kilim, late nineteenth century.

13 Close-up showing repetitive triangular pattern in each of three large, diamond-shaped medallions.

14 Close-up showing smaller subsidiary sawtooth pattern of a minor medallion.

15 On floor—Persian kilim, early twentieth century.

16 On floor—American Indian rug (Navajo), twentieth century.

17 On wall—Kurdistan pile rug, late nineteenth century.

18 On floor—Persian Sarouk pile rug with typical red ground, ca. 1920.

19 On floor—Pakistani copy of Princess Bokhara design pile rug of very recent vintage.

20 On floor foreground—Moroccan kilim with three major diamond medallions, relatively new.

     On floor background—Moroccan kilim with intersecting stepped motif, also new in age.

21 Close-up of design in background kilim pointing up the various border patterns in detail.

22,23 Close-up of kilim in foreground illustrating the designs in the field.

24 On floor—Moroccan kilim, twentieth century, with stylized stars in tile-shape squares.

25,26 Close-up of previous flatweave illustrating vibrant octagonal stars in repetitive design.

27 On floor—Eastern European kilim of recent vintage with striking ivory ground.

28 On floor—American oval rag rug of little age.

29 On floor—Soviet Russian copy of Princess Bokhara design pile rug of recent date.

30 Close-up of previous rug showing multiple borders at one corner in detail.

31 On floor—Persian Sarouk pile rug, ca. 1920.

32 On floor—Persian Soumak kilim in overall Aubusson rose pattern, twentieth century.

33 On floor—Soviet Russian copy of Princess Bokhara design pile rug of recent date.

34 Close-up of previous rug at one corner illustrating multiple borders.

35 Close-up of Soumak kilim to follow, showing detail of center medallions.

36 Close-up of Pakistan Bokhara to follow (38), showing border details at one corner.

37 On floor—Persian Senna kilim, late nineteenth century, superb example.

38 On floor—Pakistani copy of Princess Bokhara pile rug of recent date.

39 On floor—Indian pile rug in Persian design of recent date.

40 On floor right—Persian Kerman pile rug of little age.

     On stairway left—Persian Himalayan runner of recent date.

41 On floor—Anatolian prayer pile rug, late nineteenth century.

42 On floor—Oriental straw rug, twentieth century.

43 On floor—Persian Heriz pile rug, ca. 1930.

44 On floor—Persian Tabriz pile rug of recent date in animal hunt design.

45 Indian hanging.

46 On floor—Rumanian kilim, twentieth century.

47 Close-up of primary and secondary borders at one corner illustrating birds and sense of